BURNING HORSES

Poems from the Heartland

by Mathew Snyder

Copyright © 2025 Mathew Snyder

All rights reserved. No part of this book may be reproduced or transmitted in any form or by any means, electronic or mechanical, including photocopying, recording or by any information storage and retrieval system without the written permission of the author, except where permitted by law.

ISBN: 978-1-7355793-2-0

First Edition: October 2025

For Angie Obermiller

CONTENTS

The Coyote..7
Panopticon..8
Homeland..9
The Fifth Fire...10
Sawtooth...11
Warm Blooded Animals...12
Anagapesis...13
Reincarnation..14
Counting Stones..15
Letters to White Cloud...16
Winter Mud...17
Ballad of a Well Digger..18
Burning Horses...20
Outlaws..21
Unwanted Wilderness..22
Surrender to the Angel...23
Fifty-Fifty..24
Resurrection...26
Imperfection...27
After the Flood..28
Purple Sage..30
Fatherland...31
Requiem for the Mustangs.......................................32
Autumn Rain Heads East...33
Mountain Hymn..34
Will and Testament...35
Death on the Highway...36
After the Drought..38
Necropolis...39
Heathen's Prayer...40
Know Exit..42
The Story You Tell Yourself....................................43

THE COYOTE

The coyote
comes down
from the mountain
gray as the dawn
wretched, mangy

His loneliness is hunger
the growl within him
rises not from the wisdom
of his solitude
but from the thinness
of his laughter
his sorrow is thirst

His tail dances
in a way that says
to coyotes everywhere
we need the rain

PANOPTICON

In the rolling panopticon of God's country
starlings swarm like exhaled smoke
from the mountains to the plains
now comes October

Signal the warden, the rancher at the borderline
where manure-scented air demarcates
that his cattle on the hard pack
are lazing down for rain

A thunderhead comes off the mountain
erected like a scarecrow, a self-made man
returning to the wicked east
to spill out all his guts

Keening cicadas play the rhythm of the plain
blanched corn thirsting for far clouds
low on the horizon where the moon
awaits in ambush

Listen for the wisdom that comes
the transcendent revelation that comes
if it comes
in the sameness of the days

HOMELAND

Dust drifts like smoke
at dead man's curve
down in the bottomland,
river gnawing at the edges
and swallowing the road signs

My homeland rises
like pie crust on the stove
and out there in the fields
the cricket choir wails
tricked by the eclipse

I wonder how we got this far
from the river and the bridge
from rye bread on the table
from rained-soaked earth like soot
from salt and pepper, just right

Jesus, say something, won't you?
I'm in the garden alone
and the river's rising still
take your name from their mouths
and let the crickets sing tonight
their Billie Holiday lullaby

THE FIFTH FIRE

The first fire was a rolling pin.
Tornadoes up the Cimmaron.
I passed a town in Osage land
that was no longer there.
Just twisted hay rakes,
not even smoke.

The second fire was a chainsaw.
Milton made matchsticks
of the seaside Mucky Duck
where I saw dolphins
who must have been watching
paradise lost.

The third fire was an avalanche.
Rolling tides came up from the gulf.
Good old Ashville got forty days
and forty nights all at once.
And now we hardly
remember.

The fourth fire was revenge
for ever thinking eat the rich.
Lidia, Eaton, Hurst, Palisades,
Kenneth, what is the frequency?
We know it happens
every year.

The fifth fire is a highwayman.
A tricky man with an alibi
and lust for gold who tells me:
Don't believe your lying eyes,
you see, it's not piss
it's rain.

SAWTOOTH

I can't recall the horse's name
so I'll just call him Sawtooth
a ragged old gelding and small
prone to mischief and biting
no one ever said my memory was kind

This Sawtooth was a follower
maybe he got tired of assholes
or nine-year-old me on my high horse
urging him toward a swayed back
up in the Black Hills playing cowboy

He had a knack for low branches
look, Sawtooth was a bit of a bastard
like the time he kicked Jack's horse
right in the chest, a buckskin twice his size
Jack cursed that little Napoleon

Sawtooth's owner was Smitty, himself a relic
who liked to proclaim to anyone listening
faster horses, younger women, and older whiskey
somehow Sawtooth misunderstood all that
no one ever said he was like whiskey

WARM BLOODED ANIMALS

Rock-runner, searcher
round shapes, hard edges
soothed and torn
surged and ripped
red thread all at once

Sky-turner, bounder
you lose track of time
at a rock and roll bar
with uneven floors
a flea market crowd
Saturday half-drunk
remembering new faces
under slate skies
chasing rebound rain
slick roads long laid
far from home

Sooth-seeker, seek
at the water's edge
yearn to dive in
for pieces of brass
the fate of missing girls
rejuvenating mud
drowned towns lost
an end to your yearning
for the meaning of meaning
bring it back to us
and let us be

Muster warm blood
to make sense of things
as we must

ANAGAPESIS

She'd undress
slow and beguiling
when he came to her
exuberant and prideful
together they'd gasp
hands clasped
like a solar eclipse
like the moon
had eloped
with the sun

She deserted him,
bored of her quarry
a trickster, a maleficent
cat eating a nightingale,
and his threads unraveled
he hung one from
a Tuesday zenith sun,
a galactic plumb line
whose shadow pointed south
to show him the way
like a vaquero of old
longing for old Mexico
atop his Appaloosa

They plodded along
a pine tree trail
and saw the horizon
saw a wanton sun's
ominous heat shimmering
from a grotesque earth
that no moon could soothe

Originally appeared in Poetry Potluck, 2023

REINCARNATION

Her hair was thick as switchgrass
long fingers, hard hands clutched
when we walked we walked for flat miles
shared our reincarnated pasts
she had lived in Oklahoma as a skittish bobcat
I had run in Iowa rivers a box turtle
then a possum playing dead a while
she forgave me for all that without asking

One autumn night I built a fire
we stayed together quiet
wondering at our future selves
maybe sandhill cranes or mayflies
how she'd keep those sea green eyes
the woodsmoke lurking heavy in her hair
and how I would know her by her iron grasp
if we ever crossed paths again
in the slow and icy river's glide

COUNTING STONES

74 degrees
resplendent June
three bags of gravel
one of crushed rock
set the first stone
that cracked in two
said god damn it
two or three times
then set another
twice cut hands
four stones placed
three caps atop
this meager wall
holds back the dirt
of 49 years

LETTERS TO WHITE CLOUD

I'm lost on familiar roads again
I'm making notes, ink swept
I'm lost in letters reeling far behind
cranky morning sounds calling
fulsome currents, spun out east
thinkers thriving larger than their footprints
far from where my roads run straight

I'm lost in envy, desperate in doubt
while these fast-feasting Easterners
who wouldn't know this isolation
from a sinkhole in the limestone
between Pawnee territory and Sauk river paths
Meskwaki ground gone cold, I'm lost
the rivers out here swell, quarterly reporting
like ox bows, like heavy yokes on humped backs
my disbelief drowning in flood waters
is there anyone coming up the flow?
anyone at all who'll listen?

Listen! I can hear the cracks emerging
through chicken wire and spit and mud layered on
nothing in this meets expectations
I'll get out while and if I can
head east or west but still find my way
like Black Hawk, crazy like a fox
gone away and lost down the river
to trade words with White Cloud

WINTER MUD

Last year about this time
when it was nine below
my neighbor's water main burst
so the city brought in trucks, a backhoe
and they dug it out until midnight
that winter mud splattered on snow
like a film noir murder scene
I watched them all night long
from my room off the patio
and listened to records

Last summer they dug it all up
every house on down the street
got secret pipes and sprayed on grass
finally something we had in common
besides not talking to one another
and our heartfelt lack of ambition
to eradicate dandelions

BALLAD OF A WELL DIGGER

They came out of Missouri
with a forgotten name
something ancient
like a founder of Rome
if Rome was benign
or like a John Ford movie
with sons and daughters
not looking for trouble

One of those sons
the one with green eyes
and thin disposition
had a cocksure distaste
for water witching
he dug down and found
himself waiting for noon
with the notable exception
of murky days

This son, he climbed out
once his eyes had adjusted
and in dire need of a drink
he saw what he had was gone
the bed frame, the cast iron,
the stowed away cash
hell, even the Labrador

His daughter asked him
if he had any regrets
about where he had dug
his reply came uneasy

If I went deeper down
I might have drowned
but I'm not blameless
not even in the dark
I sure hope she finds
whatever it is
she's running from

BURNING HORSES

They couldn't reach the horses
hear them, yes, consumed in smoke
their shrieking children-cries

You can imagine their desire
to run across the prairie
a way illuminated from behind
to flee from their possessors
somewhere quiet and long
to be forgotten

OUTLAWS

In our old man's dreams we are outlaws
our faces masked, dust in our hair
coffee grounds, tin cups, pine smoke
at night we talk about the money
how far it will stretch us to the coast
we listen for scavengers afoot

In our old man's dream we run easy
the blanch white plain rolls on forever
ups and downs like rippled milk
the Cheyenne are ghosts behind us
the money divisible by our number
and we never wake up to frostbite

In our young man's dreams we are lawmen
chasing our quarry across the divide
we wear out our horses, get sick in the river
just what is it we're doing out here anyway?
this endless dream driven by destiny
I'll be damned if it's one we chose

UNWANTED WILDERNESS

This wilderness goes on for years
in thickets and creek runs
up these fingerling hills
there are a thousand paths among a million trees
and each a burgeoning disappointment
for there is only one way through
the way I came alone
one way through unwanted wilderness
to flawed frontiers lurking
past oak and elm and juniper
the fearsome bones of sycamores
night howls of owls and elk
to terrify my nightmare mind
there is no knowing
which and how many sermons I'll defy
or who will love me as I stray
no knowing my disappointments
save my interest in trees
and far better that they embrace me
as I stumble past searching
for my deliberation

SURRENDER TO THE ANGEL

Disassemble me, my bones
     my blood and brain and nerves

Take my scalp and let it bleed
     like a mask of red serene

Steal from me these words
     and string them around your neck

Take my second guess
     and double down to death

Take the spiders from my eyes
     weaving occulted motes

Spin my delusions as your own
     be drunk with their guilt

Strip me of everything, of land
     of every belief, of my golden memory

Let your tongue speak no more
     these words you wear as trophies

Take my charcoaled heart
     and let it warm your winters

Let the smoke into your lungs
     and take my haunted scent with you

Take my hands and lead me
     to your hidden home

FIFTY-FIFTY

In the cut of this life I have frayed
I am all loose ends
where my beard has grayed
it went gray in strands
some mornings I cannot swallow
a sting from sternum to wrist
hurt that was not always there
I am a marionette hung from nerves
pulling at my arms and eyelids
to relieve some tension ignored

I saw a picture of myself dancing
remembered strings tugging at my legs
and what it felt like inside to dance
as though guided by other hands
cheery warm from well tequila
to see my puppet-self now
I see my rough and awkward limbs
my knees pulled in two directions
lifeless in the image but not still
little puppet-strings inside gone slack
but through them I lie now
in judgment of such joy

On silver streams my children call
when I hear them I remember
how they learned to tie their shoes
cross over, wrap around, pull tight
we remain connected for a while
and I think for them
go far, hold tight
until I have to let them go
I find a string around my finger
I must have put it there
I wonder why?

That question mark hangs like a rope
with a knot at its tail
at the end of your rope, they say
tie a knot and hold on
who are they?
what the hell do they know?
how much longer now?
how much longer?
I am dancing on the inside

Looking back I see a common thread
here we all are tied to the ground
you and me and them connected
we are struck keys sustained
by vibrating piano wire
let's hold tight to good and bad
let the wire cut into our hands
so we know that all our blood is red

RESURRECTION

Sand and gravel laid bare for the dredgers
Mud sun-cracked
a septuagenarian's skin
heron tracks as Sanskrit wisdom
hidden along the shoal

When the water swells again
it will come in quietly
slithering unseen, engorged
from recent rains that come
as sudden as Cain rose up
to wipe away the tale
of what the heron knew
before he took flight:

The river won't always be like this

IMPERFECTION

They say
imperfection
runs in your family
like a black thread
in a Navajo blanket
so your spirit
can break free

AFTER THE FLOOD

I turned north at Le Claire on 97
a highway obscure to forget you by
driving against the Mississippi flow
and its river towns that run long and narrow
towns like folk songs, succinct and free
Princeton and Shafton and on into Clinton
towns that rhyme with themselves
that shed miraculous light on murky waters
but they were beset with disaster
pumping the Mississippi back into itself
they had their locks wide open
to sickly green floods like dysentery
curdling at their back doorsteps

I saw a game in the bottom of the eighth
I saw a dark egret with a wild eye like a curse
I saw every green Iowa can put forth
full-spectrum green up in dairy country
July corn like a quilt, green brilliant and dark
I saw green ivy crawling skyward on
a hundred brick facades and wondered what they were
I saw a speckled fawn dead on a curve
I saw a woman selling honey in the sun
I saw the highway ahead of me
miles and miles in a canyon of trees
I saw the surging aorta of America
pumping its nitrates into the gulf

I saw graffiti on great bridges that said
GOD IS LOVE but it was crossed out
and instead it said LOVE IS DEAD
so I thought to myself, defeated:
Eat your wretched heart out, Friedrich Nietzsche,
I'm going to Illinois where the greens
won't make me weep for the weary past
Cryin' won't help you
prayin' won't do you no good
but I couldn't hold back the flood

When I came back I saw our future
a fat old king snake eating its tail
keeping itself company, full on retributions
our fortune written in its green-black scales
spelled out in solitary profundity
poetry right at the tip of a forked tongue
but lonely was all I could remember
when I heard you calling in hotel dreams

PURPLE SAGE

She adored him like violets
her namesake bloom, simple
in May while they flourished
his color blindness a dull irony
blind as he was to redness
he took people's word
how she looked in crushed velvet
the unusual shade of her eyes
the flush skin at her throat

She loved Prince
for him it was Hendrix
they orbited one another in rhythm
she bought him sharpened knives
a heliotrope box of cards
they warmed one another
deep in December

By May she went back out west
he dreaded the distance
the heat, the endless miles of sage
he plucked violets at the cemetery
and laid them out on the patio
by August he forgot them drying there
he had his knives, his box of cards, his Hendrix

He kept things hidden
a war-wounded heart
very little left of a bottle of Crown Royal
Prince on repeat

FATHERLAND

He had been a farmer and now seemed lost on earth
his heart poured in concrete
cured in half-light
despite his protestations
he was incurious at its shape
each ventricle laid heavy, distorted
the forms that cast it
rusty irons reinforcing
sturdy as a Sunday, a plinth
pulsing in unison with a far, external choir

He adored his children having been to El Salvador
in his prime, rebar drilled into him
heart set against the Communists somehow
he taught them the value of edification
and the evils of fluoride
he leaned on such half-illuminations
sure comforts against the vanishing soil
Iowa dirt after lazy rain
black as blood clots
deadly in the lungs and brain
the steady, rigid heart
this too he ignored until his children washed away

He could not hear them
over the background television noise
when they called home

REQUIEM FOR THE MUSTANGS

The trackless prairie heaves and cries
The highway slices through
Night's weighing heavy on my eyes
A nightmare hewn in two
I'm weary of this dream
And thin on gasoline
I've only heard what she had seen
Still echoing, I hope

Out west coyotes took the night
The mustangs are all gone
Their driving lust gave way to blight
Earth empty as a yawn
Grass giving way to sand
Dust falling from my hand
I am no longer in command
But holding fast to hope

The setting sun blinds my way
A nuclear horizon
If I'm running from the day
I'm not the only one
I'm looking for some place
Darkness upon the face
Of the deep without a trace
Not too far down, I hope

AUTUMN RAIN HEADS EAST

The slow death of autumn declares itself with thunder
Not what you expected awaiting splendor and rouge
You called it Indian summer, but felt queasy saying so
You long for old ease, without ache when you sleep
The thrill of cool evening, with your bonfire memories
Ashes clinging to your jacket like first kisses

What you love is falling
What you love is dying slow
What you love is past

The susurrus of dry leaves, the hiss of a treacherous rain
Wind in the craggy trees, tilted ruins waving goodbye
Thunder fades eastward in the smallest hour
Your history scrawled in receding mud

MOUNTAIN HYMN

Listen to the mountain
not the echoes bleating
on its precipitous hide
but the mountain
itself humming
its rise and
its fall

The stone sings out our future
bone dust ground hard pan
hardpan to broad plateau
plateau to rocky foothill
foothill to slope
slope to peak

The implacable mountain
knows only two fears
the ice in the valley
and time

Let us drink cool waters
from the valley's deep
and toast to fear

WILL AND TESTAMENT

When I am gone
desecrate my grave
with whiskey and pencils
I should be so lucky
to be remembered
at all let alone
for two great vices

Or do me one better
burn me to nothing
and spread my ashes
so I might get caught
in some bastard's eye
you'll know the one
insisting you're free

DEATH ON THE HIGHWAY

I'm driving Dad down Highway 92
not to be confused with old Highway 92
which winds broken and crooked around
the folds of Marion County's lost strip mines

It occurs to me he's the last of his kind
and I think, well god damn it,
he's forgetting the way home
so Mom and I remind him where to

Remind him we're going to bury his sister
what's left of the clan, old friends I never met
some of them dead and gone and almost forgotten
hanging from the wall, suspended in sepia

The night before by stubborn candlelight
we spent the evening recalling why it was
that these old timers never went by their names
That's just what people did, Mom says

Ramona, Dad's sister, had no middle name
so she picked Vivian, which suited her fine

Everyone knew Mom's dad as Dick,
no one called him Charles Arthur

Everyone called his brother Jim,
but he was really Morris Alonso, who knew?

Another brother was Fid, but named Loel,
Fid's twin was was Lola; she married five or six times

Pat was the youngest, named Patrick Crusoe
so called by his brothers after the novel

Amos was Yag; Donald was Shorty
Dino was Cookie; a good boy who drowned in the river
Cyrus was just Cyrus; a great name and a prodigious cusser
Jonesy was Lloyd Jones; he faked his own death

Buster Converse, whose name was maybe Chuck,
well, Buster crashed his car into the tavern
got out and asked Zeke Wilson for a drink anyway
I couldn't make this all up if I tried

I'll tell you what else Mom tells me
while riding down her beloved Highway 92
we shouldn't wait more than three days to bury the dead
Death is an inconvenience, she says

AFTER THE DROUGHT

I stayed home for you and tended the parched earth
We asked for more than this when dreaming big
Ornamental grasses, roses like cabernet sauvignon
Stones from the river where I learned to name fish
That good loamy dirt gone from our memory of rain
All signs saying this is who we are now, just wait

There is no rain in this story, no perennial contenders
I moved the rosebush three feet, gave up on the grass
No lustrous quartz find among the gray river stones
There is no end to us thirsting from dreaming big
Save your consolations, I can't drink good luck or bad
When rain comes, it will be more than I can take

NECROPOLIS

I know the way like an addiction
    scrimshaw streets, bands of horses

Running hard, drawn by salt
    lured by water heavy with limescale

Under hard light I lose sight of them
    searing, harsh light the last of its kind

A light that eats color and steals words
    from my mouth sun blind and dumb

When dark creeps I stand in a crowd
    night blind and lost but I hear them

Draw in each other mumble and laugh
    a clamor of kinship unabashed by night

Would that I spoke primeval tongues
    or how to sign here is what I'd say

Do you know anyone who still knows how
    to get to 49th and Lazarus Street?

HEATHEN'S PRAYER

I have learned your language
now learn mine

Begin with curses, you'll have no choice
blessings come harder

They are a cup of dissolved sugar
sipped in stony silence

Don't you think I'd change this
if only I knew how?

To the cicadas' litany in August
their life and death whirring
to the infinite quiet of snowfall
to rattlesnake clatters of oak leaves
to rain patter, far off coyote heckles
to a lone barn owl's chant

Bring me words from from Homer
about going home

Lull me to sleep with the end
of all doubts

Cut open my ribs with the laughter
of transgression

Oh vanity, vanity, all is vanity
to borrow a phrase

When I call, I call to no one
I beg for patience

When I stand, I stand alone
to hear the future

As comfortable as the womb

KNOW EXIT

This is exactly how Harry Houdini died!
I think to myself staring down the slope
preparing my escape from predeterminism.
There's a key right at the tip of my tongue
that tastes like new blood.

Can I beat a Calvinist at cards?
I don't feel bad dealing from the bottom.
After all, what choice do I have?
I'll be damned, it's the suicide king again,
high as a mountaintop.

Geronimo! I'm rolling off of here.
Tell Houdini I don't want to disappear,
just a getaway before the sun goes down.
I'm coming down to pick another path
and leaving the resistance.

THE STORY YOU TELL YOURSELF

I had a dog
a toothbrush I liked
soft bristled, surgical
somewhere along the way
no matter what the kids say
I forgot her name

I took up a new hobby
I've been at this for a while
escape artistry
forgetfulness
photosynthesis
cliff hanging

I lived with spiders
had Mason jars for glasses
regular mouthed and lidless
apropos for a hermitage
to keep the pests away
don't you think?

I wish I could take
all of your troubles away
the barbed wire you tied
around your own necks
every last god damned
one of you

ABOUT THE AUTHOR

Mathew Snyder is a graduate of the University of Iowa. His poetry examines the shrinking nature of Midwestern life and landscape and the internal challenges of age and manhood among the hidden complexities of flyover country. Subscribe to his poetry on Subtack:

https://mathewsnyder.substack.com/

www.ingramcontent.com/pod-product-compliance
Lightning Source LLC
Chambersburg PA
CBHW030536080526
44585CB00014B/966